Backyard Animals
Ravens

Christine Webster

Weigl Publishers Inc.

Published by Weigl Publishers Inc.
350 5th Avenue, Suite 3304, PMB 6G
New York, NY 10118-0069
Website: www.weigl.com

Library of Congress Cataloging-in-Publication Data

Webster, Christine.
 Ravens / Christine Webster.
     p. cm. -- (Backyard animals)
 Includes index.
 ISBN 978-1-60596-082-1 (hard cover : alk. paper) -- ISBN 978-1-60596-083-8 (soft
cover : alk. paper)
 1. Ravens--Juvenile literature. I. Title.

 QL696.P2367W43 2010
 598.8'64--dc22

                                          2009004175

Printed in China
1 2 3 4 5 6 7 8 9 0 13 12 11 10 09

Editor Heather C. Hudak
Design Terry Paulhus

All of the Internet URLs given in the book were valid at the time of publication.
However, due to the dynamic nature of the Internet, some addresses may have
changed, or sites may have ceased to exist since publication. While the author
and publisher regret any inconvenience this may cause readers, no responsibility
for any such changes can be accepted by either the author or the publisher.

Photo Credits
Every reasonable effort has been made to trace ownership and to obtain
permission to reprint copyright material. The publishers would be pleased
to have any errors or omissions brought to their attention so that they may
be corrected in subsequent printings.

Weigl acknowledges Getty Images as its primary image supplier for this title.

Arizona Sonora Desert Museum, Photographed by Lisa M Brashear, 2005:
Page 7, bottom left; Christof Asbach: Page 7, top right; Lip Kee: Page 7, top left;
Ron Co -Tasmania: Page 7, bottom right

Contents

Meet the Raven

Ravens are glossy-black-colored birds. They have a long, slightly curved beak, a wedge-shaped tail, and strong feet. The feathers on their throat are long and shaggy.

Ravens easily **adapt** to new environments and climates. They live in many parts of the Northern Hemisphere. Ravens are found in North America's hot deserts, cold mountains, and **temperate** forests. They also live in Europe, Africa, and Asia. Ravens are part of many legends, folklore, and stories from these parts of the world.

Ravens are often found in small groups or pairs. In wintertime, they will gather in large groups. Often, this is done near food sources.

Fascinating Facts

Ravens often can be seen rolling and somersaulting through the air. Sometimes, they fly upside down for about 0.62 miles (1 kilometer).

Some ravens can copy
the sound of a human voice.

All about Ravens

Raven is the name given to about 10 types of birds that belong to the crow family. Common ravens are the most familiar of these birds. They are the largest of all the songbirds, at about 22 to 27 inches (56 to 69 centimeters) long.

Common ravens are the largest all-black birds in the world. They have sharp eyesight and excellent hearing. These birds are very smart. In fact, they are thought to be some of the most **intelligent** birds. They can **imitate** many different sounds, including the human voice.

Common ravens weigh about 24 to 57 ounces (680 to 1,616 grams).

Where Ravens Live

Brown-necked Raven

- Lives in the eastern parts of North Africa and the Middle East

Thick-billed Raven

- Found in the mountains and high plateaus of Eritrea, Somalia, and Ethiopia

Chihuahuan Raven

- Found in Mexico and the southwestern United States

Forest Raven

- Lives in southeastern Australia and Tasmania

Raven History

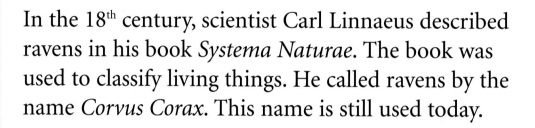

Ravens have been on Earth for a long time. The earliest **fossils** of birds similar to ravens are millions of years old.

In the 18th century, scientist Carl Linnaeus described ravens in his book *Systema Naturae*. The book was used to classify living things. He called ravens by the name *Corvus Corax*. This name is still used today.

Over time, ravens have settled near humans. In some places, these birds are thought to be pests. Programs have been put in place to decrease their numbers. In other places, there are few ravens. In the early part of the 1900s, ravens nearly disappeared from the northeastern United States. These areas have programs to bring ravens back.

Common ravens can make 15 to 33 different sounds.

In nature, ravens live about 10 to 15 years. Ravens that are under the care of humans can live more than twice as long.

Raven Shelter

Ravens live in many types of **habitats**. They make their homes in thick forests, on prairies, and in deserts and canyons. Some ravens live along the sea coast. Others make their homes on farmers' fields, small towns, and busy cities.

Ravens like to build their nests in high areas. This can include cliffs, large poles, or tall buildings. Ravens first look for a platform to place their nest. Then, they begin building their nest out of sticks and twigs. The sticks and twigs are woven into a basket shape. Inside, ravens line the nest with layers of mud, fur, bark, grass, and paper.

Ravens can live in places that have cold weather. This is because their black feathers absorb heat.

Ravens are strong fliers.
They can hover in one place
or soar high in the air.

Raven Features

Raven bodies are made for flying and catching **prey**. They can live in many climates and parts of the world. They have many features to help them do these things.

SOUND
The raven's call is a deep croaking "rrronk" sound. The bird makes other sounds that are similar to knocks and a ringing bell.

BILL
A raven's bill is long and slightly hooked. The powerful bill can crack open seeds or pull apart tough **carrion**.

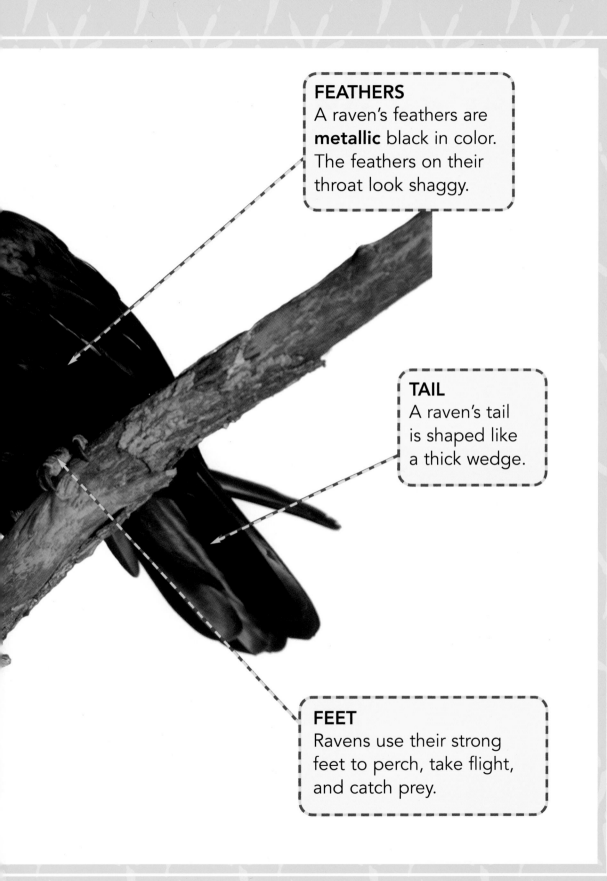

FEATHERS
A raven's feathers are **metallic** black in color. The feathers on their throat look shaggy.

TAIL
A raven's tail is shaped like a thick wedge.

FEET
Ravens use their strong feet to perch, take flight, and catch prey.

What Do Ravens Eat?

Ravens are **omnivorous**, but they mainly eat meat. They hunt small animals, such as mice, snakes, lizards, and birds. Ravens also eat eggs, bugs, grains, berries, fruit, and garbage. They usually find their food on the ground, but sometimes ravens will look for food in trees.

Ravens are **scavengers**. They fly overhead looking for carrion. When ravens spot a **carcass**, they land near it. Then, they hop forward or sideways to the carcass to eat it.

Sometimes, ravens work together to find food.

Before landing near carrion, ravens look for other birds, such as blue jays and crows. If these birds are at the site, then ravens know the area is safe from danger.

Raven Life Cycle

Ravens mate when they are between three and four years old. Once they choose a mate, ravens stay together for life. The female raven lays her eggs in a nest that is built on a bridge, cliff, tree, building, and large pole.

Eggs

A raven lays about three to seven eggs at a time. The eggs are a greenish blue with streaks and spots of brown. The male raven feeds the female while she keeps the eggs warm.

Babies

Baby ravens hatch after about 20 days. They have no feathers. They are sparsely covered in **down**. The male brings food to the nest for both mother and babies. After four to seven weeks, the babies will fly out of the nest. They stay close for a few more weeks. Then, they are ready to live on their own.

Both parents help feed the young. To feed their babies, the parents **regurgitate** their food and water from a pouch in their throat.

Adults

At night, ravens travel in flocks and **roost**. Before dawn, the group divides, as ravens search alone or in pairs for food. Ravens usually travel about 30 miles (48 km) a day in search of food.

Encountering Ravens

Ravens are a common sight in the skies around cities, towns, and in the country. Many birdwatchers enjoy sighting ravens. They like to hear their "cawing" and other sounds.

Some people think ravens are pests. They can harm farmers' crops, cause power failures by damaging power lines, and scatter garbage. Ravens have even pecked holes in airplane wings and stolen golf balls.

Sometimes, a raven may become injured. Babies may fall out of the nest, or an adult may fly into a window. If you find an injured raven, contact a local wildlife office. Place the raven in a cardboard box, and keep it in a safe, warm place.

Useful Websites

To learn more about ravens, check out www.desertusa.com/mag99/ oct/papr/raven.html.

Unlike many other types of birds, ravens do not migrate. This means they do not fly to warmer climates during the winter.

Myths and Legends

Different cultures have many legends, stories, and poems about ravens. Often, ravens take on the role of a thief, cheater, or a trickster in these tales. Many western cultures use the raven as a symbol of death, danger, and wisdom.

Some American Indian stories tell how the raven is the creator of Earth, the Moon, the Sun, and stars. Other tales claim that some animals, such as the raven, could act like humans. They were said to be spirit guides.

American Indians in Alaska believe the raven brings the daylight each day.

Owl and Raven

According to an Inuit legend, the raven was not always covered with black feathers. This is the story of how the raven changed color.

At one time, Owl and Raven were good friends. Raven made Owl a black-and-white dress. Then, Owl made Raven a pair of whale-bone boots. Owl also began to make a white dress for Raven. One day, Owl asked Raven to come for a dress fitting.

As Owl tried to work on the dress, Raven became restless. After a while, Owl became angry and shouted at Raven to stop moving around. However, Raven did not listen. Owl was very upset and tossed the blubber from a lamp on Raven. This turned the dress black. From that day on, Raven was black in color.

Frequently Asked Questions

What is the difference between a common raven and a crow?

Answer: Common ravens are almost twice as large as most crows. They grow to about 24 inches (61 centimeters) long, with a wingspan of about 4 feet (1.2 meters). Crows are only about 18 inches (46 cm) long. Ravens have long, shaggy feathers on their throat and a short, thick beak. Crows have smooth neck feathers and a long, thin beak. Ravens have a wedge-shaped tail, while crows have a fan-shaped tail.

Do male and female ravens look alike?

Answer: Both male and female ravens look the same. The only difference is their size. A male raven is slightly larger than a female.

Do ravens have predators?

Answer: Ravens have no known natural **predators**. Hawks, eagles, and owls, and coyotes may try to steal raven eggs, but they are often chased away by an adult raven.

Puzzler

See if you can answer these questions about ravens.

1.   What do ravens eat?
2.   How does a female eat while nesting?
3.   How many sounds can ravens make?
4.   How do ravens feed their young?
5.   What roles do ravens usually take in legends?

Find Out More

There are many more interesting things to learn about ravens and other birds. If you would like to learn more, look for these books at a library near you.

Bradley, James V. *Crows and Ravens.* Chelsea House, 2006.

Herkert, Barbara. *Birds in Your Backyard.* Reader's Digest, 2004.

Words to Know

adapt: to adjust to new conditions

carcass: the remains of an animal

carrion: dead animals

down: soft, sparse feathers

fossils: traces of an animal that are left behind in rocks

habitats: natural living places

imitate: to copy

intelligent: very smart

metallic: very shiny

omnivorous: to eat both plants and animals

predators: animals that hunt other animals for food

prey: an animal that is hunted for food

regurgitate: to bring food back into the mouth after it has been swallowed

roost: the place where birds rest at night

scavengers: animals that will eat foods they can find easily in their surroundings, especially dead animals

temperate: a place that has mild temperatures

Index

Skateboard Stars

By K. C. Kelley

www.childsworld.com

Published in the United States of America by The Child's World®
1980 Lookout Drive • Mankato, MN 56003-1705
800-599-READ • www.childsworld.com

Thanks to Jim Fitzpatrick for making sure
we made all the right moves.

ACKNOWLEDGMENTS

The Child's World®: Mary Berendes, Publishing Director

Produced by Shoreline Publishing Group LLC
President / Editorial Director: James Buckley, Jr.
Designer: Tom Carling, carlingdesign.com
Cover Design: Slimfilms

Photo Credits
Cover–Corbis
Interior–AP/Wide World: 7, 16; Grant Brittain 8 (3); Corbis: 5, 10,
11, 14, 15, 19, 21, 23, 27, 28; Getty Images: 6, 13, 18, 24, 26; iStock: 29.

LIBRARY OF CONGRESS CATALOG-IN-PUBLICATION DATA

Kelley, K. C.
  Skateboard stars / by K. C. Kelley.
    p. cm. — (Reading rocks!)
  Includes index.
  ISBN-13: 978-1-59296-861-9 (library bound : alk. paper)
  ISBN-10: 1-59296-861-9 (library bound : alk. paper)
  1. Skateboarders—United States—Biography—Juvenile
literature. I. Title. II. Series.

  GV859.812.K45 2007
  796.220922—dc22
  [B]

                              2007004205

CONTENTS

MEET THE
Stars!

High above the crowd, a skateboarder stands at the top of a ramp. As the fans chant his name, he takes a deep breath. Looking down into the deep wooden pit below him, he stomps on his board and drops in!

Zooming back and forth in the U-shaped **vert ramp**, he soars into the air each time he gets to the top. Like a gymnast, he spins his body in amazing ways. The board seems to be glued to his feet. The crowd screams and yells for more.

With a last awesome flip, he lands, skidding on his knees to the bottom of the ramp. His board clatters away. The sound is drowned out by the cheers of his fans!

Skateboarding is one of the hottest sports around. New stars are coming along to join longtime heroes. Let's take a ride with the superstars of skateboarding.

Tony Hawk was born with the right name. When he steps onto his skateboard, he can practically fly. Since starting with his first board when he was nine, Tony has become the most famous skateboarder ever.

Tony and his dad Frank set up a mini-ramp in their California garage.

Tony grew up near San Diego, California. He was a bit of a "wild child." He says he was full of energy and always looking for the next fun way to play. "I was a rail-thin geek on a sugar buzz," he writes on his Web site.

Everybody Into the Pool

Tony and other skaters in the 1970s got their start in swimming pools. No, they weren't swimming—the water was drained out. But the curving shapes and high walls of the pools made for great places to practice. Those same shapes were later used to make today's skateparks.

Tony took to skateboarding like a fish to water. By the time he was 14, he was a **professional** skateboarder. According to the experts, Tony was the best skateboarder in the world by the time he was 16. In Tony's pro career, he entered more than 100 events . . . and won 73 of them! He has invented more tricks than any other skater, too.

Tony rolled up the vert ramp, soared into the air and spun two-and-a-half times, then landed cleanly.

In 1995, the X Games were born. The X Games (the X is short for "extreme") feature great action sports and all the greatest athletes in those events. Millions of new fans got to see Tony. He and other amazing skaters did awesome tricks live on TV. Though he was older than most other skaters, Tony dominated. He won 10 X Games gold medals and 18 medals overall in the next 10 years.

By the time of the 1999 X Games in San Francisco, Tony was already a huge international star. At that event, he made his biggest splash yet. During the Best Trick competition, Tony rolled down the ramp, soared into the air, and twisted his body two-and-a-half-times around before landing safely.

All circles can be divided into 360 degrees, starting from zero at the top and continuing all around the circle. So 180 degrees is halfway around a circle, while 360 degrees equals the entire circle.

He had hit the 900! That number comes from two full 360-**degree** circles (720), plus half of another (180). He was the first ever to do this amazing trick. It was, he screamed, "The best day of my life!"

The Hawk flies! Tony does a "grab" move while spinning in the air off the ramp.

Tony **retired** from most competitions in 2005, but he still skates for his fans sometimes. His greatest work now—along with raising his skate-loving kids Spencer, Riley, and Keegan—is helping young skaters. Tony runs a group that raises money to build skateparks around the country.

He has also traveled to many countries to talk about skating and visit with young skateboarders. Tony's companies help produce popular skateboarding computer games, too. He has also organized the BoomBoom HuckJam action-sports show, written bestselling books, and designed skateboards and skate clothes.

The energetic little kid from San Diego now runs a worldwide skateboarding empire. But Tony hasn't gotten a big head—he still fits into his helmet! He's still having as much fun as when he was just starting out.

Tony loves spending time with his wife Lhotse and his children. Here, they're with Spencer and Keegan.

GOING FOR
Big Air

Tony Hawk is not the only high-flying skateboard star. A number of other guys have thrilled fans and made themselves famous by ignoring **gravity**. They use their creativity, skill, and courage to go for the "big air."

The king of big air is Danny Way. Here are a few of his incredible, high-flying big-air stunts:

- Danny built the world's biggest piece of skateboard equipment, the MegaRamp. It's more than 70 feet (21 m) high!

- Danny has used the MegaRamp to enter the *Guinness Book of World Records* by soaring 23.5 feet (7 m) above the ramp.
- He put the MegaRamp next to the Great Wall of China in 2005, and soared over it!

Danny's ability to fly on a skateboard is **unmatched**. He also holds records for longest distance flown (79 feet/24 m) after taking off from a vert ramp. He was also twice named Skater of the Year.

Here's Danny, in red, heading down the MegaRamp to jump over the Great Wall.

Bob's success has led many young Brazilians to take up skateboarding.

How's this for getting big air? Bob Burnquist once dropped into a 40-foot (12-m) ramp. Using it to gather speed, he then slid on a rail for 50 more feet (15 m) . . . and then fell off the edge of a cliff! Fortunately, he was wearing a parachute and had planned the fall. But it was another example of the creativity of one of the world's best skaters.

Bob grew up in Brazil and didn't start skating until he was 11. He burst onto the scene in 1995 when he won an international event against the world's top skaters. Along with his bravery in the air, he has another skill that sets him apart. Bob can ride equally well with either foot in front on the skateboard. This lets him switch back and forth between tricks with speed and ease.

Bob shows off his balance on this rail glide along the top of a vert ramp.

Along with the parachute jump, Bob's most famous trick was completing a 360-degree loop around a fully circular ramp.

Andy performs a perfect hand plant at the top of the vert ramp.

Andy McDonald is known as a quiet, serious, and pleasant person. But put him on a skateboard and watch out! Few skaters have had as much regular success as Andy in the past decade. From 1998 through 2003, he racked up the most points in the World Championship Skateboard series. Plus, Andy's 16 all-time X Games medals are second only to Tony Hawk's 18.

Andy spends a lot of non-skateboarding time talking to young people about staying away from drugs and the importance of healthy eating.

One of Andy's specialties is the vert doubles competition, which he has won five times. In this tricky event, two skaters zoom back and forth on the same ramp, trying to mesh their tricks into an entertaining ride. Andy usually rides with the great Tony Hawk in these events.

Perhaps no skater has found as much gold in the air as Bucky Lasek. With four X Games championships, he has more vert golds than anyone else. He's also taken the top vert spot in the Gravity Games and at events around the United States and the world. Plus, in 2006, he grabbed his first Best Vert Trick gold medal.

Bucky is so good on the ramp, it seems as if he spends more time in the air than on the ground.

Bucky has no fear on the ramp. He'll try any trick to gain points and amaze fans and fellow skaters. He skates very **aggressively**, using power and speed to do his moves.

Although he's been competing for more than 15 years, Bucky shows no signs of slowing down.

Another big-air skater is Cara-Beth Burnside. As a champion snowboarder, she is used to high-flying action. Cara-Beth dominates women's vert events. She won the 2006 X Games gold medal!

On snow or wheels, Cara-Beth combines creativity and amazing balance.

From the snowy reaches of Canada comes our final "big air" superstar. EXPN.com has called Pierre-Luc Gagnon "one of the best vert skaters to ever step on a board." In his first seven X Games, he skated away with seven medals—all in the Vert or Big Air competitions. He was the 2005 gold medalist.

Pierre-Luc's style combines speed with amazing gymnastic ability. "I do a lot of flip tricks in my runs," he says. "But I mix it up by doing spin tricks, lip tricks, and big airs. It's important to show people that you really have control."

Through all the big air that these stars fly, control is the key. They power their way into the air, but then it's up to them to turn, twist, flip, and spin with flair. The very best can invent brand-new tricks, too. Of course after that, all that's left is to land in one piece!

Pierre-Luc is the best skater to come from Canada.

SKATEBOARD
Hotshots

Coming on the "wheels" of today's **veteran** stars are a group of young skaters ready to challenge for best in the sport.

The first is Shaun White. Very few athletes can say that they are among the best in the world in one sport, let alone two. But that's just what the Flying Tomato can boast. Shaun, who earned his famous nickname thanks to his red hair, earned a gold medal in the **halfpipe** at the 2006 Winter Olympics. It wasn't for skateboarding, however.

Shaun made lots of new fans at the 2006 Winter Olympics.

It was for that sport's winter cousin, snowboarding.

Shaun's also an awesome skateboarder. He has won silver medals in vert competitions in Summer X Games and scored big points for his creative tricks.

On land or snow, Shaun is an ace in the air. His great balance helps him stay on whatever board he's using.

Shaun grew up near San Diego. He had two heart surgeries before he was five, but he quickly bounced back. He had a skate ramp and a trampoline in his yard, so flying high was part of growing up.

Shaun first started snowboarding when he was six. He's been a pro snowboarder since he was 12 and turned pro in skateboarding in 2003.

His body-twisting, gravity-beating skills work equally well in both sports. He thrilled Olympic fans with his gold-medal run in 2006 in Italy.

That year, Shaun became the first skater to try a 1080 . . . a half-spin more than Tony Hawk's 900. Shaun didn't land it, but the attempt put him among the world's top skaters.

Shaun's bubbly personality has made him a favorite among fans and the media.

The skaters we've met so far specialize in the vert events. However, street skaters are gaining in popularity every year. Street skaters ride over, around, through, and under objects on a course set up to look like a regular street scene.

P-Rod's dad, Paul Sr., is a famous comedian and actor.

Paul Rodriguez is a big street star, winning X Games gold in 2004 and 2005. The man they call "P-Rod" got a lot of headlines by earning the first **sponsorship** for a skater from the Nike sneaker company.

Although he's only 22, P-Rod has been skating as a pro for five years.

Elissa Steamer has a very creative skating style. She goes after all the street tricks very aggressively.

He combines aggressive skating with excellent control of his board—a must in street skating.

Elissa Steamer is the top female street skater. She has won dozens of big events, including the 2006 X Games street skate gold. In 2004, she became the first woman to be featured in a skateboarding video game.

Ryan Sheckler is only 16, but he has earned lots of medals, money, and fame for his awesome street-skating skills.

Our final hotshot is the youngest of the bunch. Ryan Sheckler burst onto the skateboard scene in 2003 when he won the X Games street competition—when he was only 13 years old!

Ryan has proved to be more than a one-win wonder ever since. In 2004, he won the U.S. Skateboarding Championships. In 2005, he captured the season championship on the Dew Tour of pro skaters. That's not bad for someone who just got his drivers' license in 2006!

Remember, all the big stars featured in this book started as young skaters.

Skateboarding continues to grow, with more and more fans around the world. Tony Hawk has (mostly) flown on, but big-air stars like Shaun White still soar. In the street, Ryan Sheckler leads a group of fearless, creative skaters. Okay, now put down the book, put on your helmet, and get skating!

GLOSSARY

aggressively   fiercely, with great energy

degree   a unit of measurement; there are 360 degrees in a circle

gravity   the force that holds all things to the earth

halfpipe   in snowboarding, a long, snow-covered U-shaped run with high, curving sides on which people ride back and forth, doing tricks

professional   a person who is paid or earns money to perform an activity, in this case skateboarding

retired   stopped working in a particular field or left a pro sports career behind

sponsorship   money paid to an athlete to represent a company's products

unmatched   like nothing or nobody else

vert ramp   in skateboarding, a narrow, high-sided, U-shaped ramp on which skaters ride back and forth, doing tricks

veteran   a person who has taken part in an activity for a long time

FIND OUT MORE

BOOKS

Skate! The Mongo's Guide
by Ben Bermudez (LPC Group, 2001)
A fun-filled book packed with skateboarding games, trivia, and tips.

Skateboarding
by Russ Spencer (Child's World, 2006)
A how-to book that can help you learn basic tricks.

Tony Hawk
by Jim Fitzpatrick (Child's World, 2007)
Learn more about the world's most famous skateboarding star.

WEB SITES

Visit our Web page for lots of links about skateboarding and skateboard stars: www.childsworld.com/links

Note to Parents, Teachers, and Librarians: We routinely check our Web links to make sure they're safe, active sites—so encourage your readers to check them out!

INDEX

K.C. Kelley has written for young readers about a wide range of sports, from baseball and football to skateboarding and NASCAR. Though he hasn't been on a skateboard himself, all the kids in his neighborhood in Santa Barbara, California, are totally stoked on the sport!